FUN FACT FILE: SPACE!

20 FUN FACTS ABOUT STARS

By Kristen Rajczak

Gareth Stevens PUBLISHING

Please visit our website, www.garethstevens.com. For a free color catalog of all our high-quality books, call toll free 1-800-542-2595 or fax 1-877-542-2596.

Library of Congress Cataloging-in-Publication Data

Rajczak, Kristen.
20 fun facts about stars / by Kristen Rajczak.
p. cm. — (Fun fact file: space!)
Includes index.
ISBN 978-1-4824-1014-3 (pbk.)
ISBN 978-1-4824-1015-0 (6-pack)
ISBN 978-1-4824-1013-6 (library binding)
1. Stars — Juvenile literature. I. Rajczak, Kristen. II. Title.
QB801.7 R35 2014
523.8—d23

First Edition

Published in 2015 by
Gareth Stevens Publishing
111 East 14th Street, Suite 349
New York, NY 10003

Designer: Sarah Liddell
Editor: Greg Roza

Photo credits: Cover, p. 1 Space Frontiers/Stringer/Archive Photos/Getty Images; p. 5 noppharat/Shutterstock.com; p. 6 NASA/Science Source/Photo Researchers/Getty Images; p. 7 nienora/Shutterstock.com; p. 8 photo courtesy of Wikimedia Commons, Solar internal structure.svg; p. 9 Michelangelus/Shutterstock.com; p. 10 Stocktrek Images/Getty Images; p. 11 Time & Life Pictures/Contributor/Time & Life Pictures/Getty Images; p. 12 Universal History Archive/Contributor/Universal Images Group/Getty Images; p. 13 NASA/Handout/Hulton Archive/Getty Images; p. 14 PHILIPPE HUGUEN/Staff/AFP/Getty Images; p. 15 Albert Barr/Shutterstock.com; p. 16 John A. Davis/Shutterstock.com; p. 17 Photo by ihsopuqak/Flickr/Getty Images; p. 18 ARCHITECTEUR/Shutterstock.com; p. 19 photo courtesy of Wikimedia Commons, Cellarius ptolemaic system c2.jpg; p. 20 nikm4860/Shutterstock.com; p. 21 photo courtesy of Wikimedia Commons, Crux (Southern Cross) from Hobart, Tasmania.jpg; pp. 22 (background), 23 (background) Standret/Shutterstock.com; pp. 22, 23 Science Museum/Contributor/SSPL/Getty Images; p. 24 Ola-ola/Shutterstock.com; p. 25 isak55/Shutterstock.com; p. 26 Michael Margolies/iStock/Thinkstock.com; p. 27 Aaron Jackson/Flickr/Getty Images; p. 29 Nick White/Photodisc/Thinkstock.com.

Printed in the United States of America

CPSIA compliance information: Batch #CS15GS: For further information contact Gareth Stevens, New York, New York at 1-800-542-2595.

Contents

Words in the glossary appear in **bold** type the first time they are used in the text.

Sky Lights

From Earth, stars look like points of light. They seem beautiful and peaceful as they shine in the night sky. But the billions of stars in the billions of **galaxies** of the universe are actually superhot balls of energy and light. Their "lives" are millions or billions of years long, and their deaths can be huge explosions!

For thousands of years, people have been studying stars' movements and makeup. Today, we know there's a lot more to stars than just pretty light!

Our sun is a star! It's the closest star to Earth.

From the Beginning

FACT 1

We can't see most stars with just our eyes.

Stars are huge **celestial** bodies. They're made of gas, and their light comes from the energy created within them. However, except for the sun, stars are **light-years** away from Earth. Most don't burn bright enough for us to see them without a telescope.

With the help of very powerful telescopes, such as the Hubble Space Telescope, more of the billions upon billions of stars in the universe can be seen.

A nebula is a giant cloud of dust and gas in space. Stars and planets are created in nebulas. Many stars form nebulas when they die.

FACT 2

Stars are born in temperatures of about 18 million °F (10 million °C) or more.

New stars form when **gravity** causes a nebula's gas and dust to clump together. As these clumps grow bigger, they spin and heat up, creating the star's center. **Nuclear reactions** begin. A star is born once it's hot enough.

FACT 3

A star is fueled by the gases hydrogen and helium.

In a star's center, or core, nuclear reactions change hydrogen into helium. This creates energy. The energy is carried away from the core through the radiation zone. Near the star's surface, the energy swirls around in the convective zone. Once hydrogen is used up, stars burn helium.

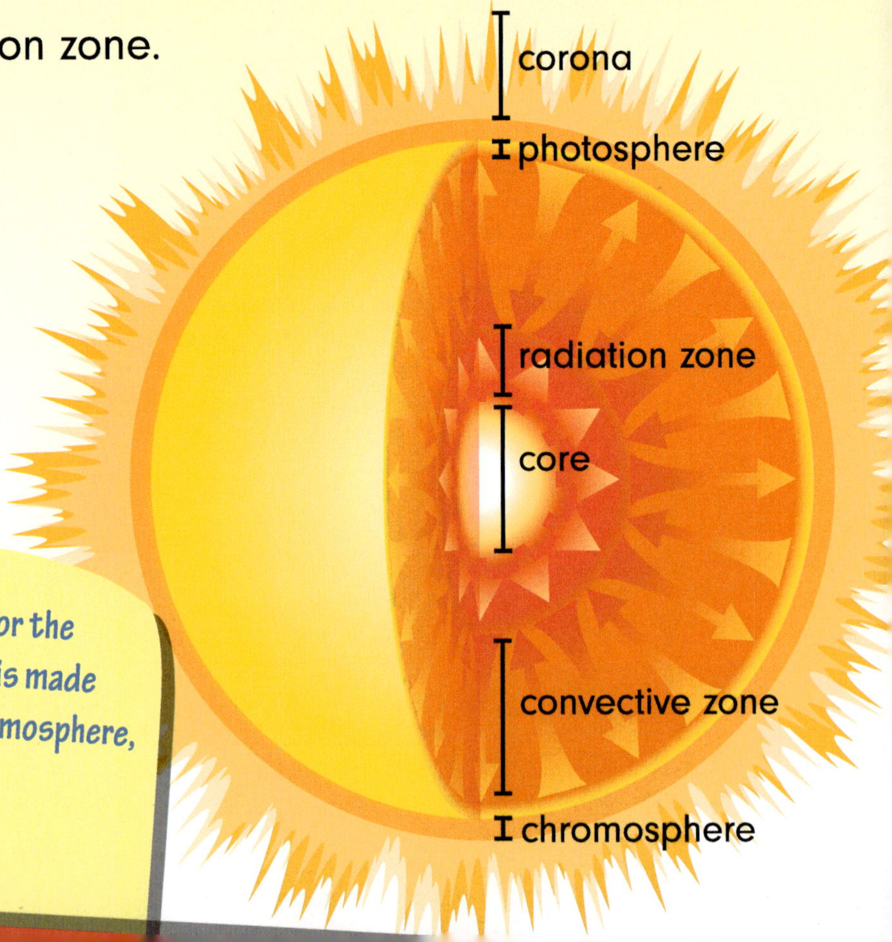

A star's atmosphere, or the gases that surround it, is made up of the photosphere, chromosphere, and corona.

Long Lives

FACT 4

The sun will continue to give Earth light and heat for all your life and long past the lives of your children.

The sun has been a main-sequence star for about 5 billion years. A star spends most of its life in this stage. It will stay in a steady state for about 5 billion more years.

There are stars much bigger and much smaller than the sun.

FACT 5

How long a star lives depends on its size.

A star's gravity pulls matter inward, while nuclear reactions send energy outward. These two forces are balanced. But the core can only burn for so long! Very large, or massive, stars burn through their hydrogen fuel more quickly than smaller stars.

What happens to a star after its main-sequence stage also depends on its size. Some huge stars grow even larger, brighter, and hotter, and may be called supergiants or hypergiants. This image shows what one might look like.

After the sun's red giant stage, it will lose its outermost layers and become a planetary nebula with a cooling core, or white dwarf, at its center.

FACT 6

Stars may die quietly—or explode!

Later in their life, stars may grow larger and turn red, becoming red giants. Once their fuel runs out, they may shrink to become white dwarfs. Massive stars have more fuel to burn, but they don't last as long. When massive stars die, they don't shrink—they blow up!

FACT 7

The dust from star explosions may eventually form other stars and planets.

The explosion of a very large star is called a supernova. For weeks and sometimes months, it's the brightest light in the sky! A supernova often leaves behind a dense, or tightly packed, core. The rest of the star drifts away into the universe.

This image shows what's left after a supernova in a nearby galaxy.

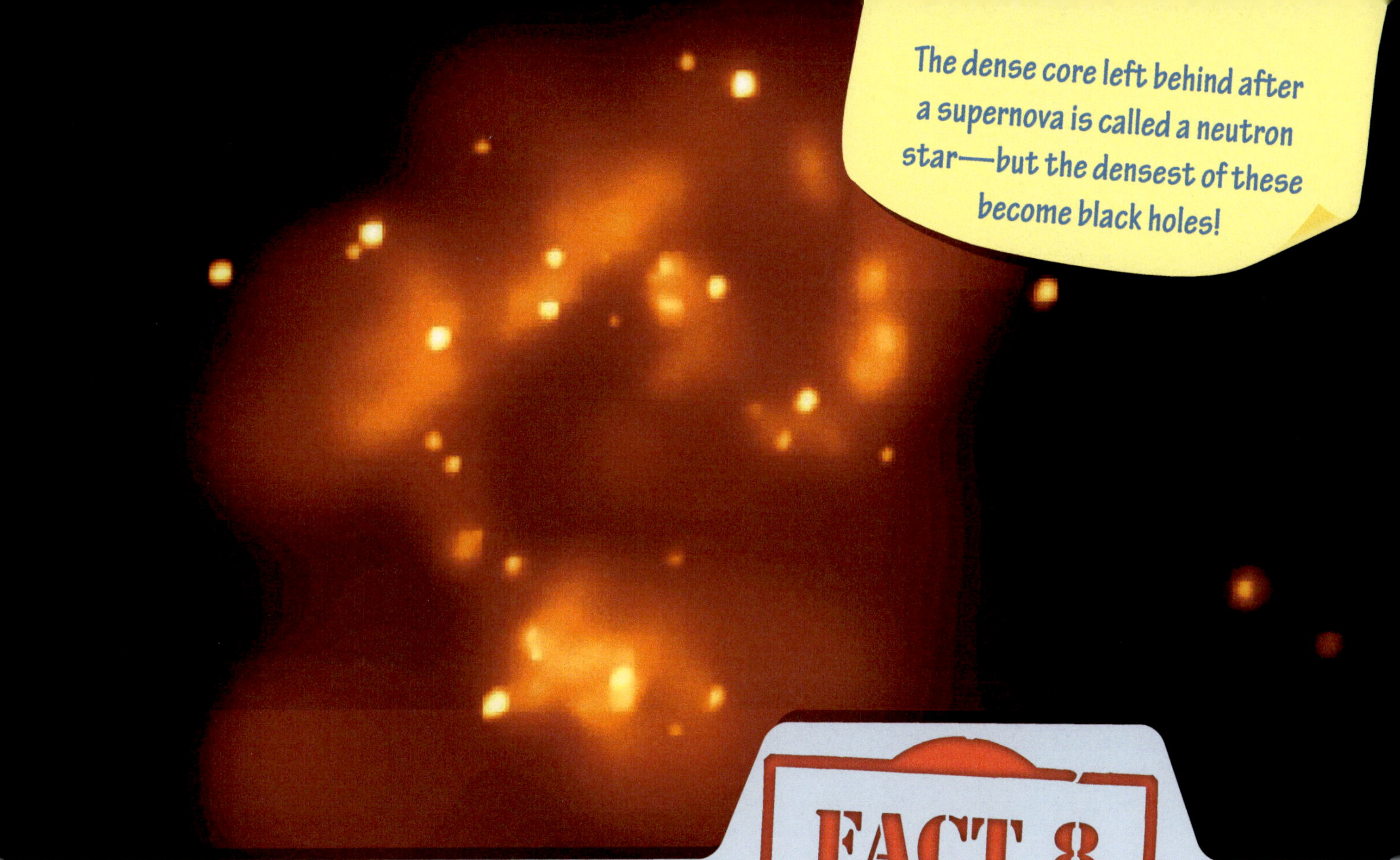

The dense core left behind after a supernova is called a neutron star—but the densest of these become black holes!

FACT 8

Black holes were once stars.

Massive stars have a huge amount of gravity. It causes them to collapse, or cave in, and explode as supernovas. The dense core left behind has such a strong gravitational pull that not even light can escape. This is a black hole!

Star Light, Star Bright

FACT 9

Scientists use a special tool called a photometer to measure the brightness of a star.

Scientists study stars' light to learn about them. They can tell a star's size, temperature, and whether it's moving toward or away from Earth. The amount of energy a star puts out, or its luminosity, is another feature scientists can learn from studying a star's light.

Scientists who study heavenly bodies are called astronomers. They may use telescopes that have photometers to observe stars.

Stars can be a range of different colors. The color of a star can also tell scientists what it's made of.

FACT 10

A star's color tells you how hot it is.

Stars' surfaces can be almost 100,000°F (55,538°C)! These superhot stars shine blue or white. Not all stars are that hot, though. The next-hottest stars look yellow, like the sun. The sun is about 10,000°F (5,538°C). Cooler stars look red.

Mapping the Night Sky

FACT 11

Trying to find a single star can be like looking for a needle in a haystack.

Constellations are groupings of stars. They make individual stars easier to find in a night sky where thousand of visible stars are shining. Spotting the bright stars in Orion's belt may help you find the star you're looking for!

If you live in North America, Orion is one constellation you might know.

FACT 12

The ancient Greeks recorded more than half of the constellations used today.

People have been stargazing for a long time! Cave paintings found in southern France possibly show groupings of stars, making the first record of constellations more than 17,000 years old! The Greek astronomer Hipparchus (huh-PAHR-kuhs) made the first star chart around 100 BC.

FACT 13

There are 88 official constellations.

In the early 1900s, there were many groupings of stars that overlapped in the night sky. The International Astronomical Union (IAU) set 88 official constellations in 1930. The constellations are defined not by stars, but by **coordinates**.

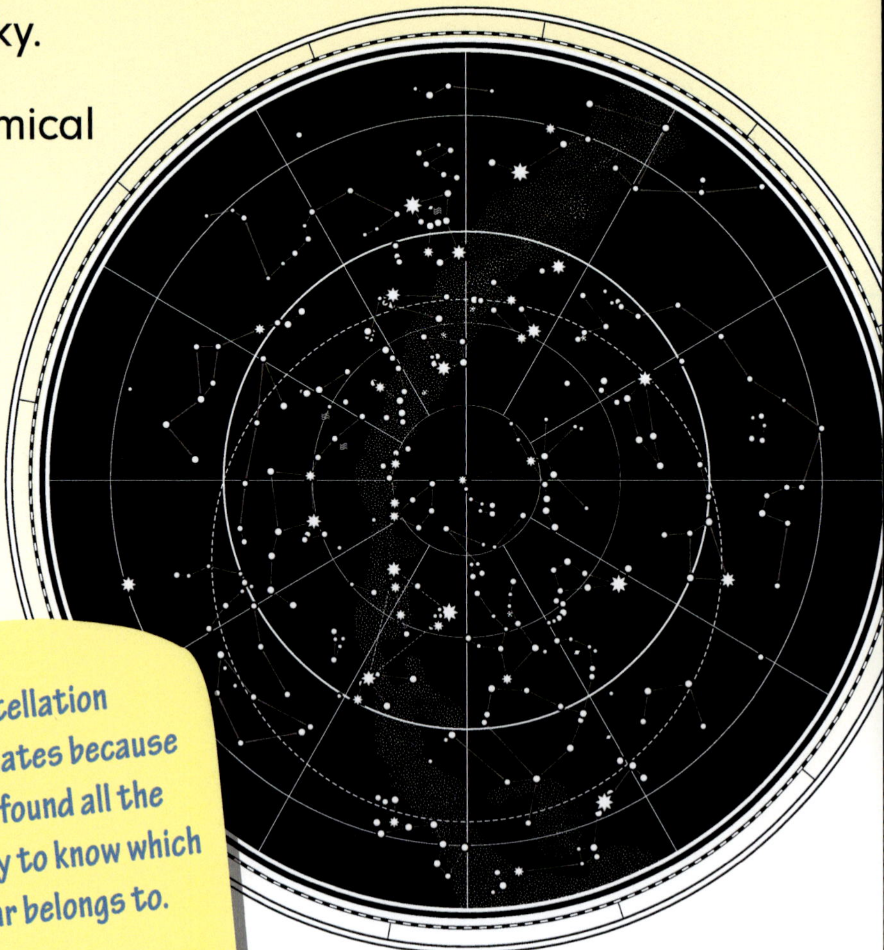

The IAU set constellation boundaries by coordinates because new stars are being found all the time. It's an easier way to know which constellation a star belongs to.

Each star has an address.

Locations on Earth can be found using **latitude** and **longitude** lines. Imagine filling this imaginary grid with air, like a balloon, so it surrounds Earth. These imaginary lines are what scientists use to map the skies.

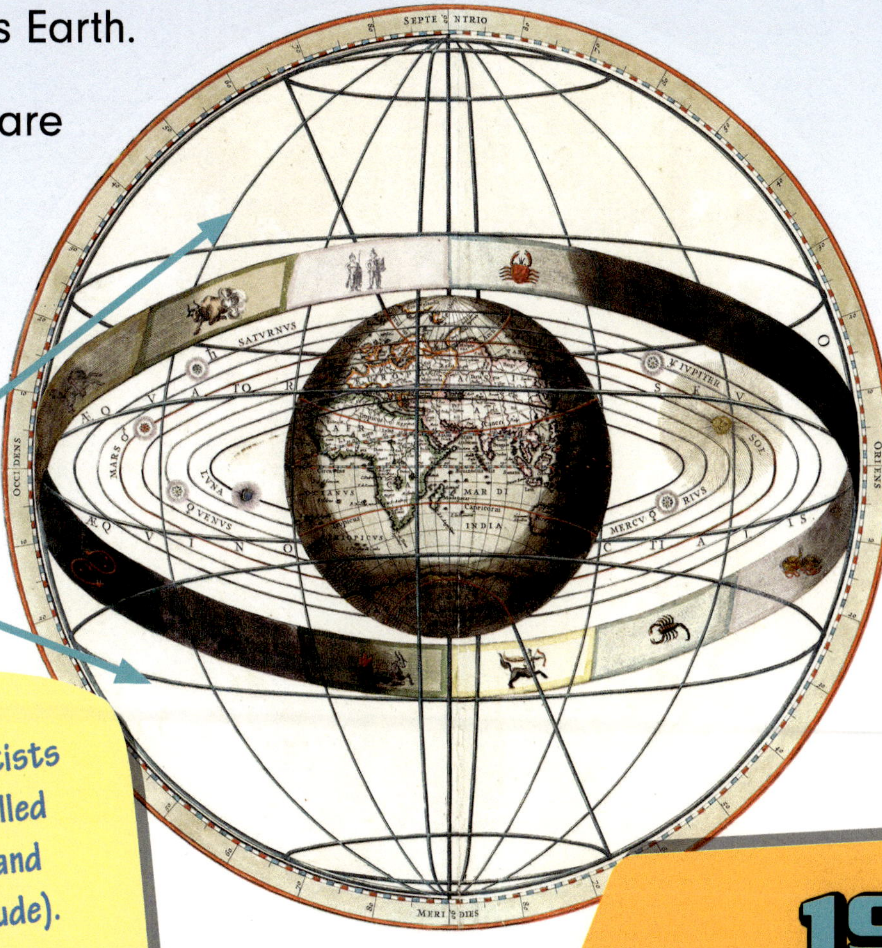

The imaginary lines scientists use to map stars are called declination (latitude) and right ascension (longitude).

FACT 15

The Big Dipper isn't a constellation.

An asterism is a commonly known pattern of stars that isn't a constellation. However, one or more of the stars in an asterism may be part of a constellation. The stars in the Big Dipper are part of the constellation Ursa Major, or the Big Bear.

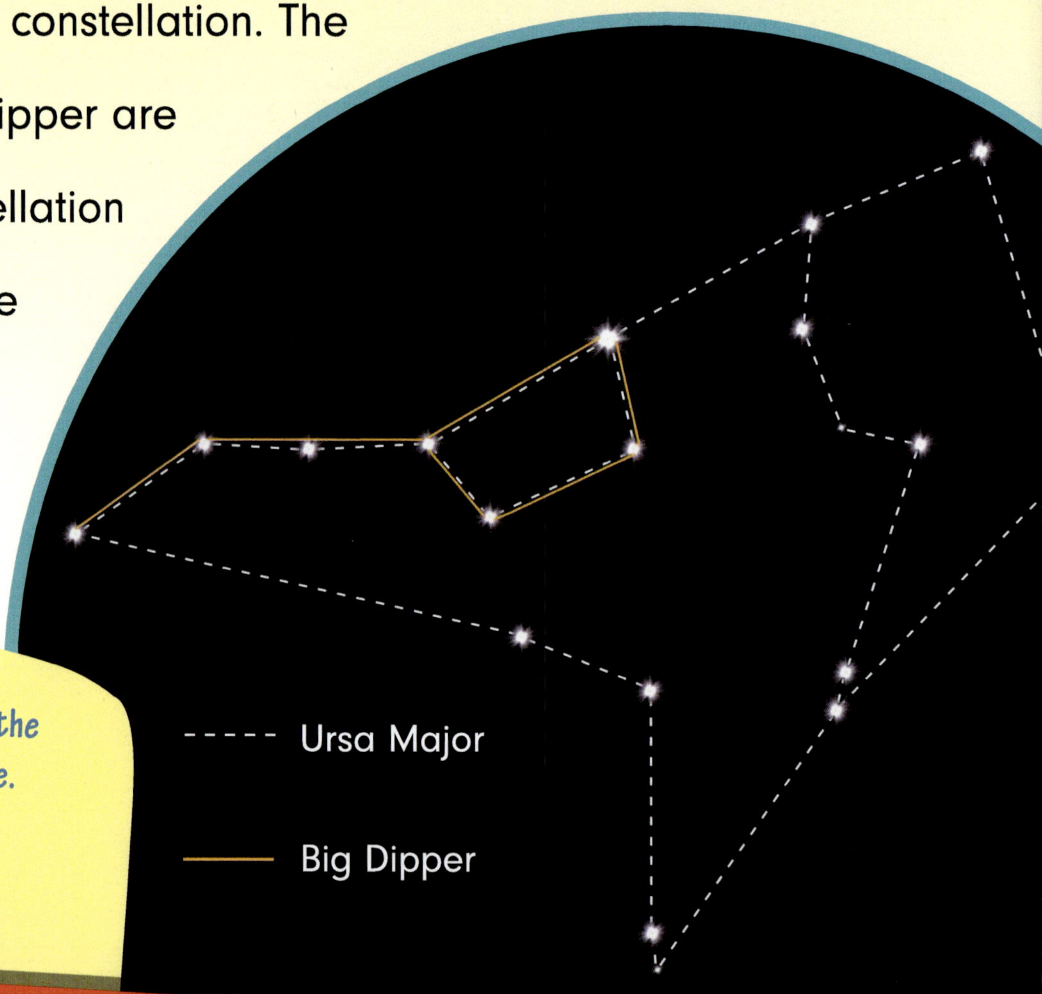

The Big Dipper is called the Plough (plow) in Europe.

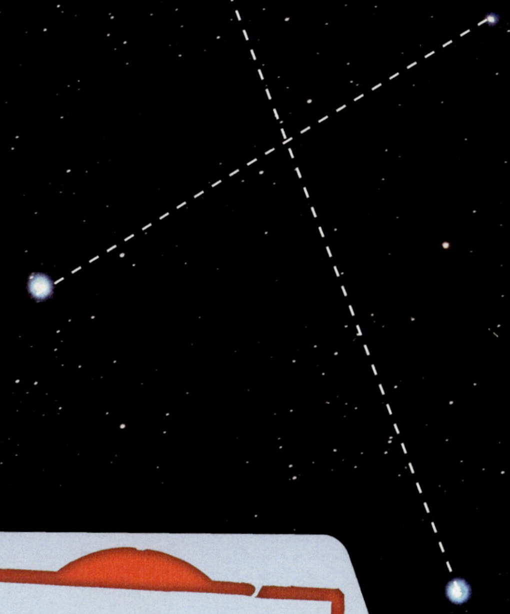

The night sky changes from season to season, too. The Southern Cross, for example, can be seen year-round in some places in the Southern Hemisphere, but only in May and June in Hawaii and northern Africa.

FACT 16

The night sky in Australia has different stars in it than the night sky in the United States.

What stars you see in the night sky depends on your latitude. Some stars that can be seen in the Northern **Hemisphere** can't be seen in the Southern Hemisphere. This is because of Earth's round shape and its movement around the sun.

Star Charts

Star charts like these show the stars and constellations seen in the night sky in the Northern and the Southern Hemispheres.

NORTHERN HEMISPHERE

SOUTHERN HEMISPHERE

Name Game

FACT 17

Some constellations are named for ancient monsters and heroes.

In the past, knowing constellations helped travelers find their way. Farmers could tell what time of year it was when certain constellations appeared in the sky. Ancient stories about the constellations made remembering them easier. Some were named after **mythical** heroes.

Twelve constellations are named for zodiac signs. A person's zodiac sign is based on their birthday.

Other constellations are more modern, such as Microscopium, which was named after the microscope.

The star Epsilon Ursae Majoris is the brightest star in the Big Dipper. It has a name that is based on an Arabic word: Alioth.

FACT 18

Stars may have more than one name.

Stars discovered long ago have Arabic names that have been used for hundreds of years. Astronomers have renamed some stars based on the constellation they're found in. As other stars are found, numbers and Greek letters have been added to names, too.

FACT 19

You can name a star after your grandmother—but it's not official.

Companies sell stars and star names. Though this seems like a nice gift, the IAU doesn't recognize these star names. When a new star is discovered, the IAU won't call it Aunt Milly—its name will probably be mostly numbers.

Giving someone a star is a cool present, even if it's not scientifically recognized.

When many meteors fall, it's called a meteor shower. Some meteor showers happen at the same time every year. They're named for the constellations they appear to come from, such as the Perseids, shown here.

FACT 20

Shooting stars aren't stars at all!

Meteors are bits of rock and space **debris** that burn up and glow as they enter Earth's atmosphere. They move at tens of thousands of miles an hour, which is why they look like they're "shooting" across the sky.

Stargazing

Planetariums are a cool way to learn more about stars. Projections of different parts of the night sky are shown above you while an astronomer or knowledgeable person guides you through space. You can also visit an observatory—such as Kitt Peak National Observatory in the Sonoran Desert—and see far into space using high-powered telescopes.

Then again, on a clear night, you and your friends or family can just look up! Find an open place where there aren't many lights, such as a park, and you can stargaze for hours.

Tell your teacher about a local planetarium. It would make a great field trip for your science class!

Glossary

celestial: having to do with the sky

coordinate: any of a set of numbers used to tell the location of a point on a line, on a plane, or in space

debris: the remains of something that has been broken

galaxy: a large group of stars, planets, gas, and dust that form a unit within the universe

gravity: the force that pulls objects toward the center of a planet or star

hemisphere: one-half of Earth

latitude: the imaginary lines that run east and west above and below the equator

light-year: the distance light can travel in 1 year. It's the unit used to measure distance in space.

longitude: the imaginary lines that run north and south on either side of the Prime Meridian

mythical: having to do with a story that isn't true

nuclear reaction: splitting or joining atoms, the smallest bits of matter, to create energy

For More Information

Books

Hunter, Nick. *Stars and Constellations.* Chicago, IL: Capstone Heinemann Library, 2014.

Rustad, Martha E. H. *Constellations.* Mankato, MN: Capstone Press, 2012.

Sparrow, Giles. *The Sun and Stars.* Mankato, MN: Smart Apply Media, 2012.

Websites

Astronomy for Kids
www.kidsastronomy.com
Play games, look at pictures, and read about all kinds of space topics.

Discovery Kids: Space
kids.discovery.com/tell-me/space
Find out the answers to many questions about space.

Publisher's note to educators and parents: Our editors have carefully reviewed these websites to ensure that they are suitable for students. Many websites change frequently, however, and we cannot guarantee that a site's future contents will continue to meet our high standards of quality and educational value. Be advised that students should be closely supervised whenever they access the Internet.

Index